ADULT PATTERNS

Coloring Book

Jasmine Taylor

Book design by Jasmine Taylor

ISBN 978-0-359-87173-5
90000
9 780359 871735

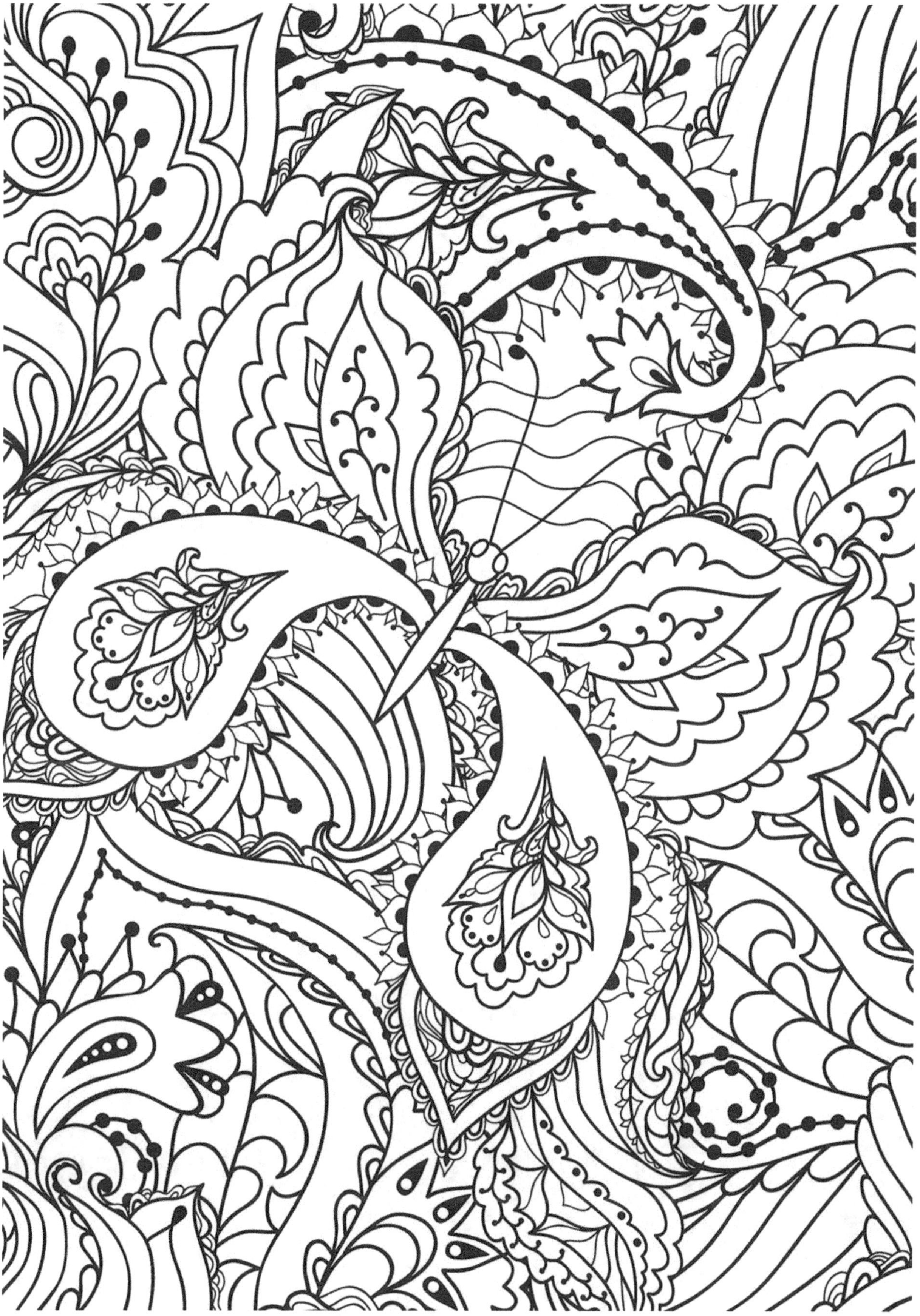

ARTIST

NAME

DATE

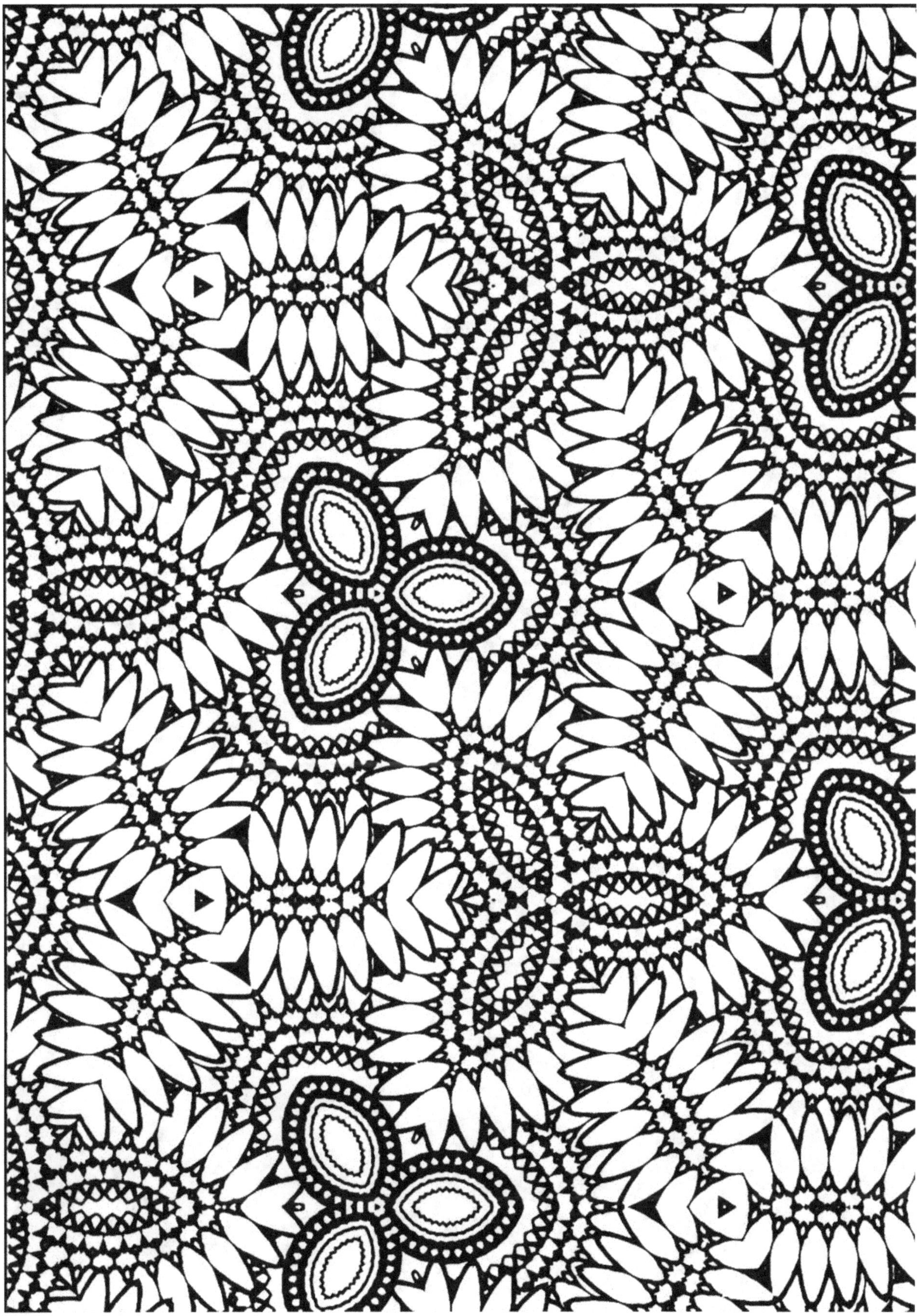

ARTIST

NAME

DATE

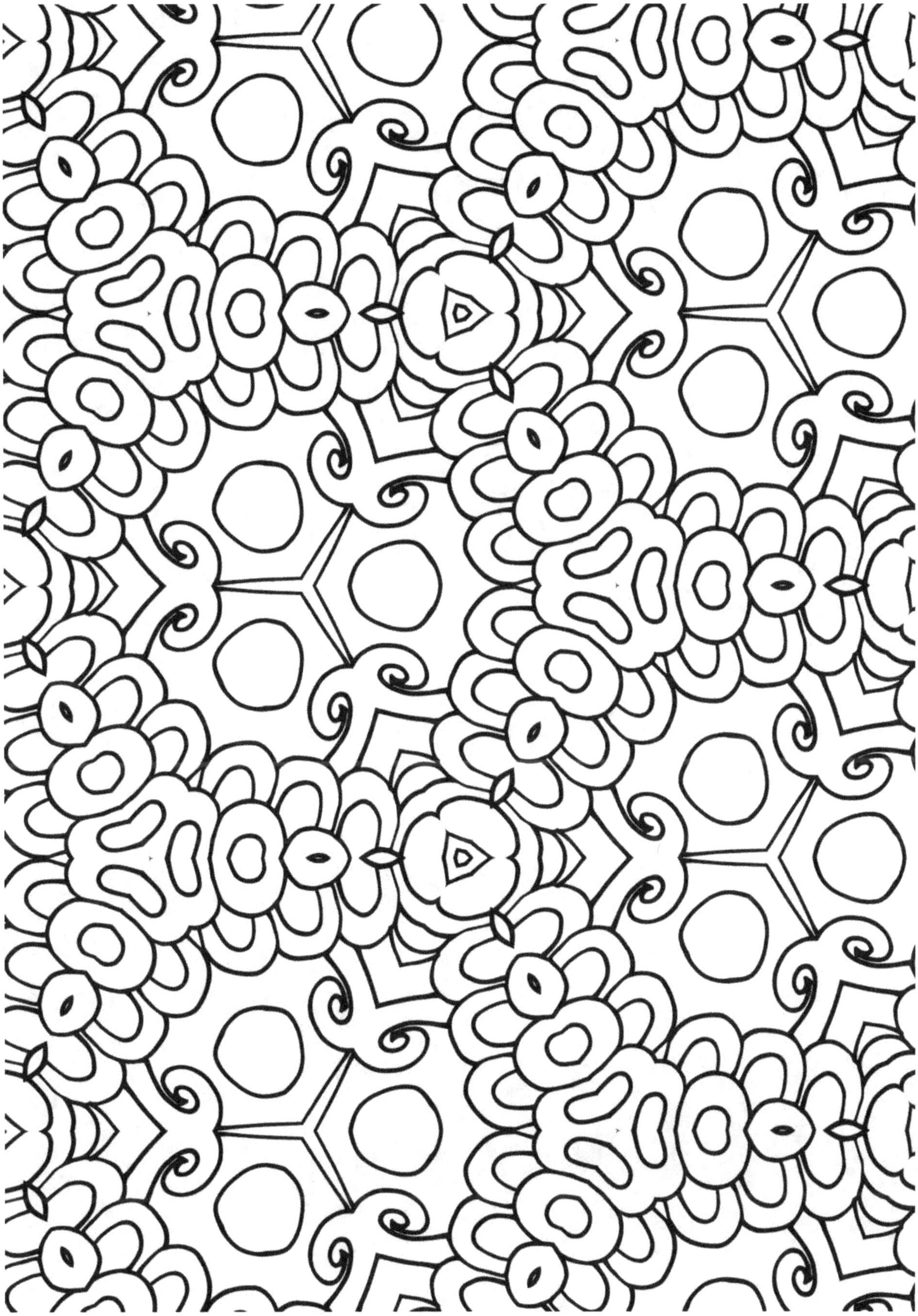

ARTIST

NAME

DATE

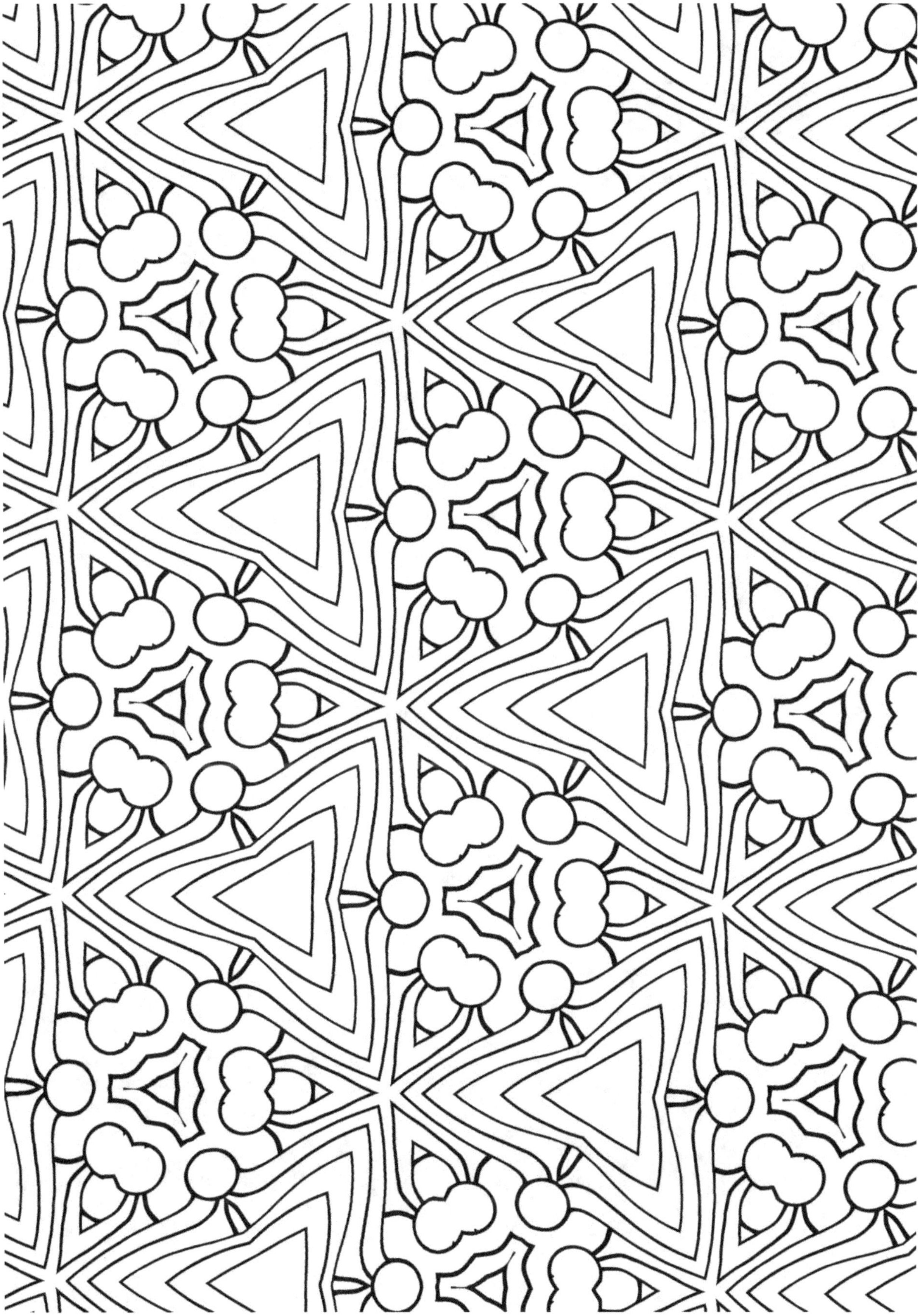

ARTIST

NAME

DATE

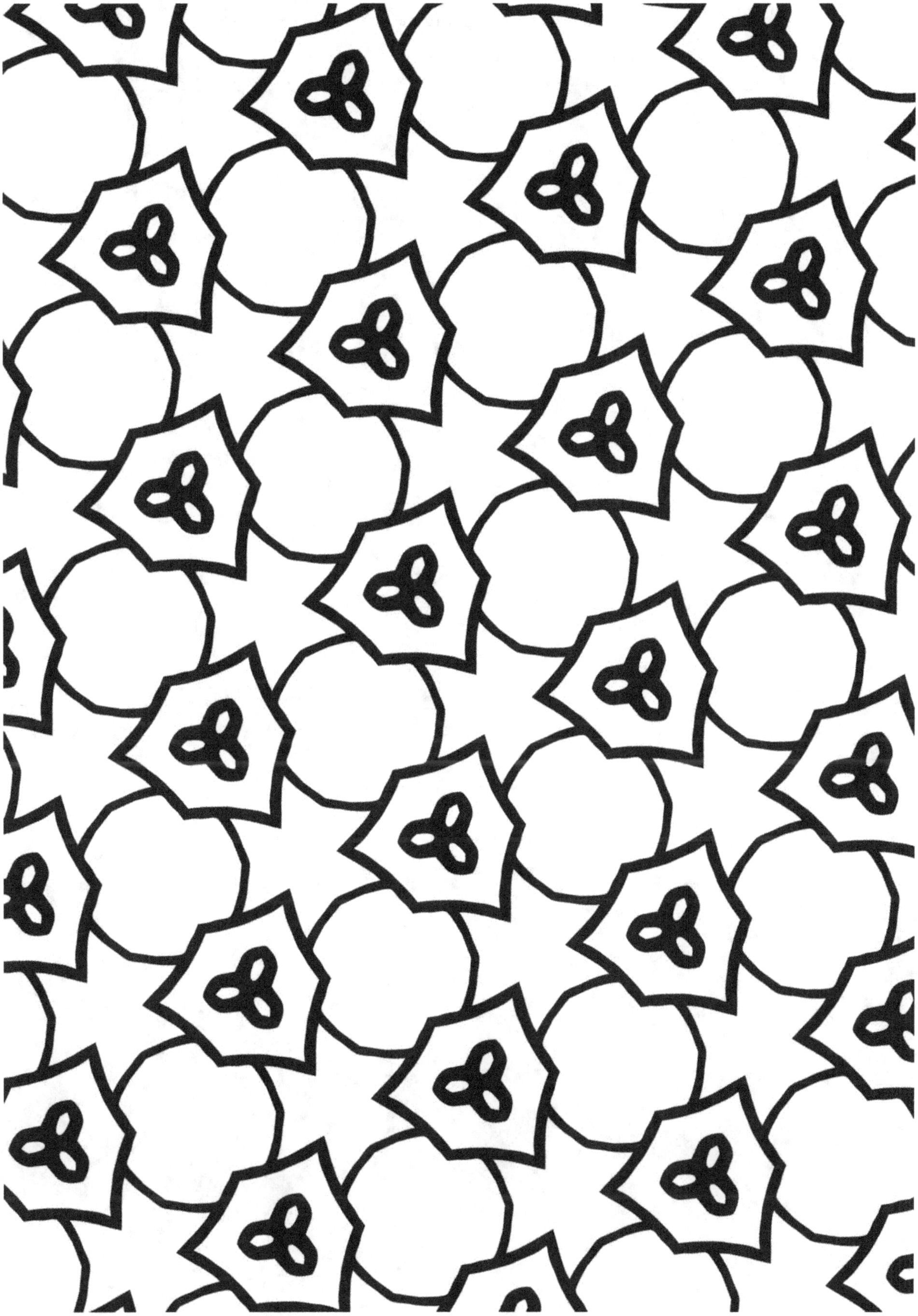

ARTIST

NAME

DATE

ARTIST

NAME

DATE

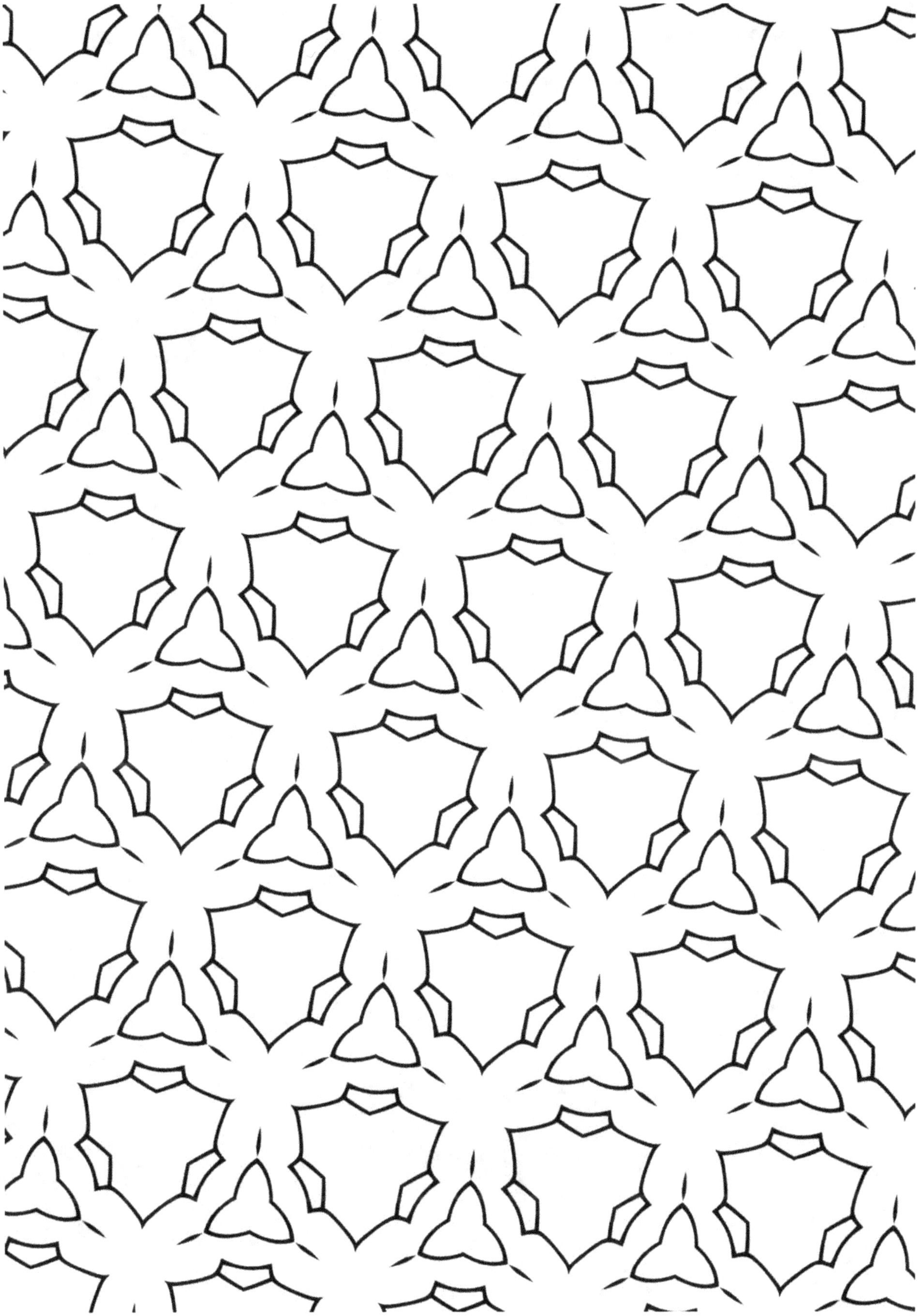

ARTIST

NAME

DATE

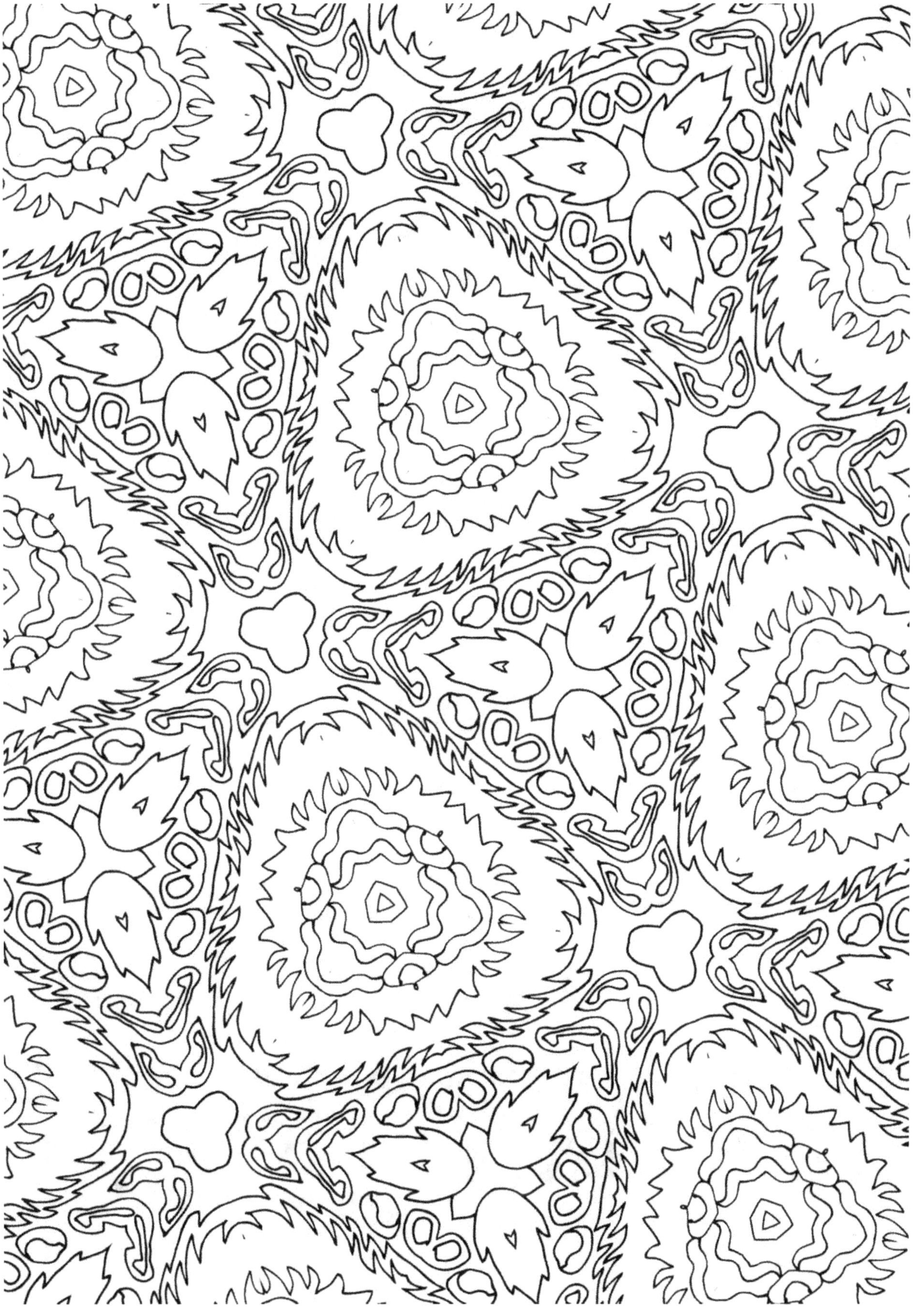

ARTIST

NAME

DATE

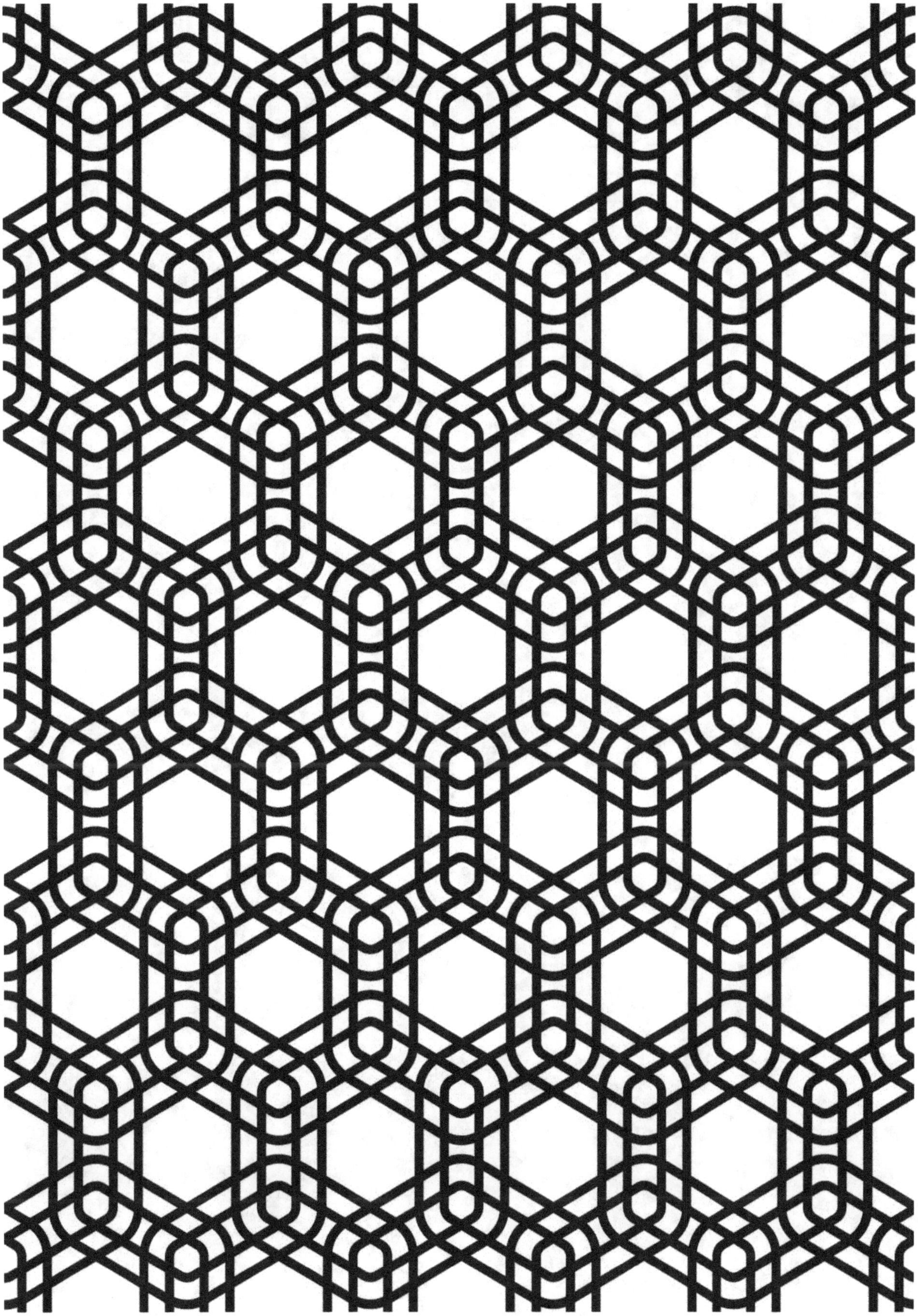

ARTIST

NAME

DATE

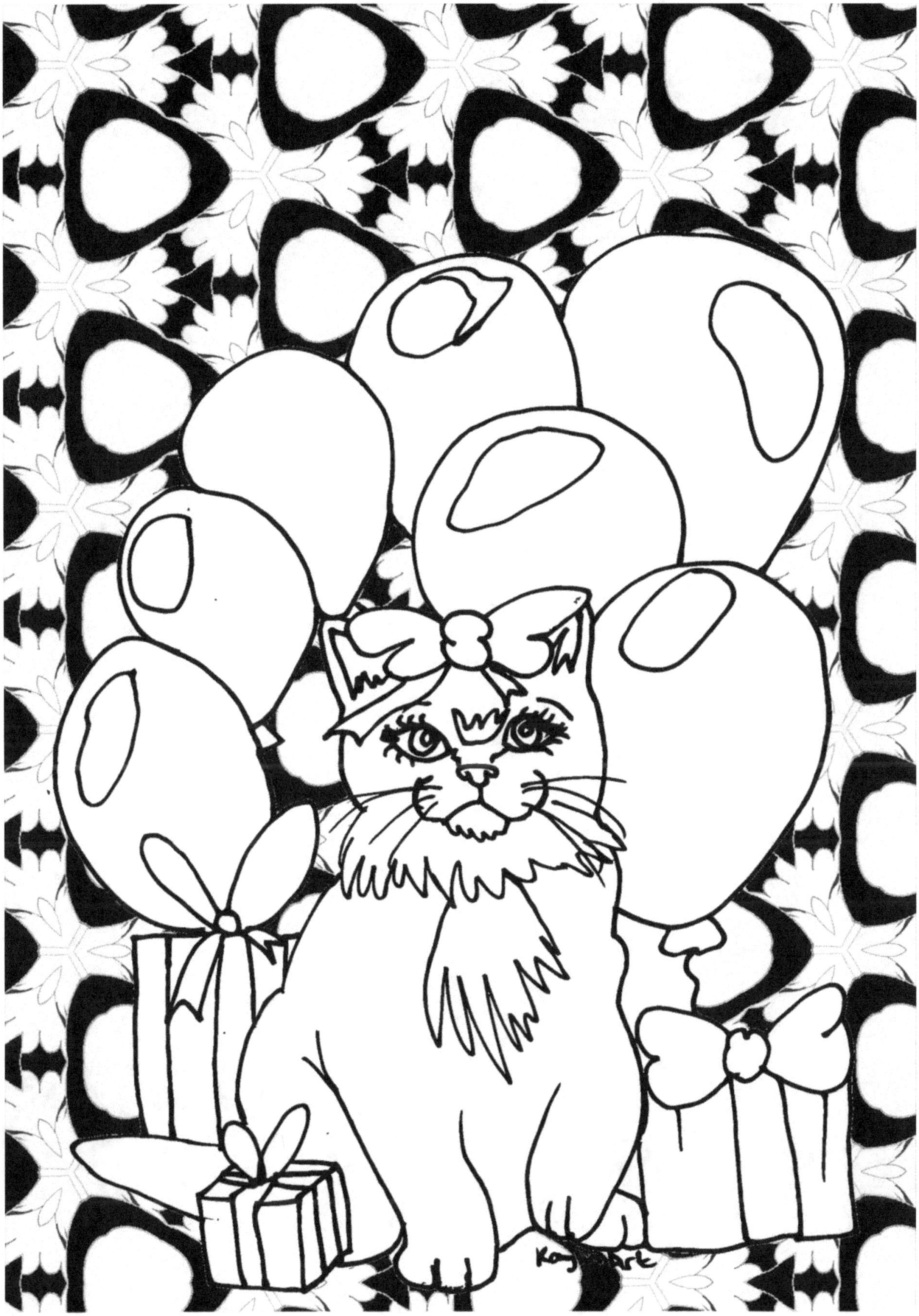

ARTIST

NAME

DATE

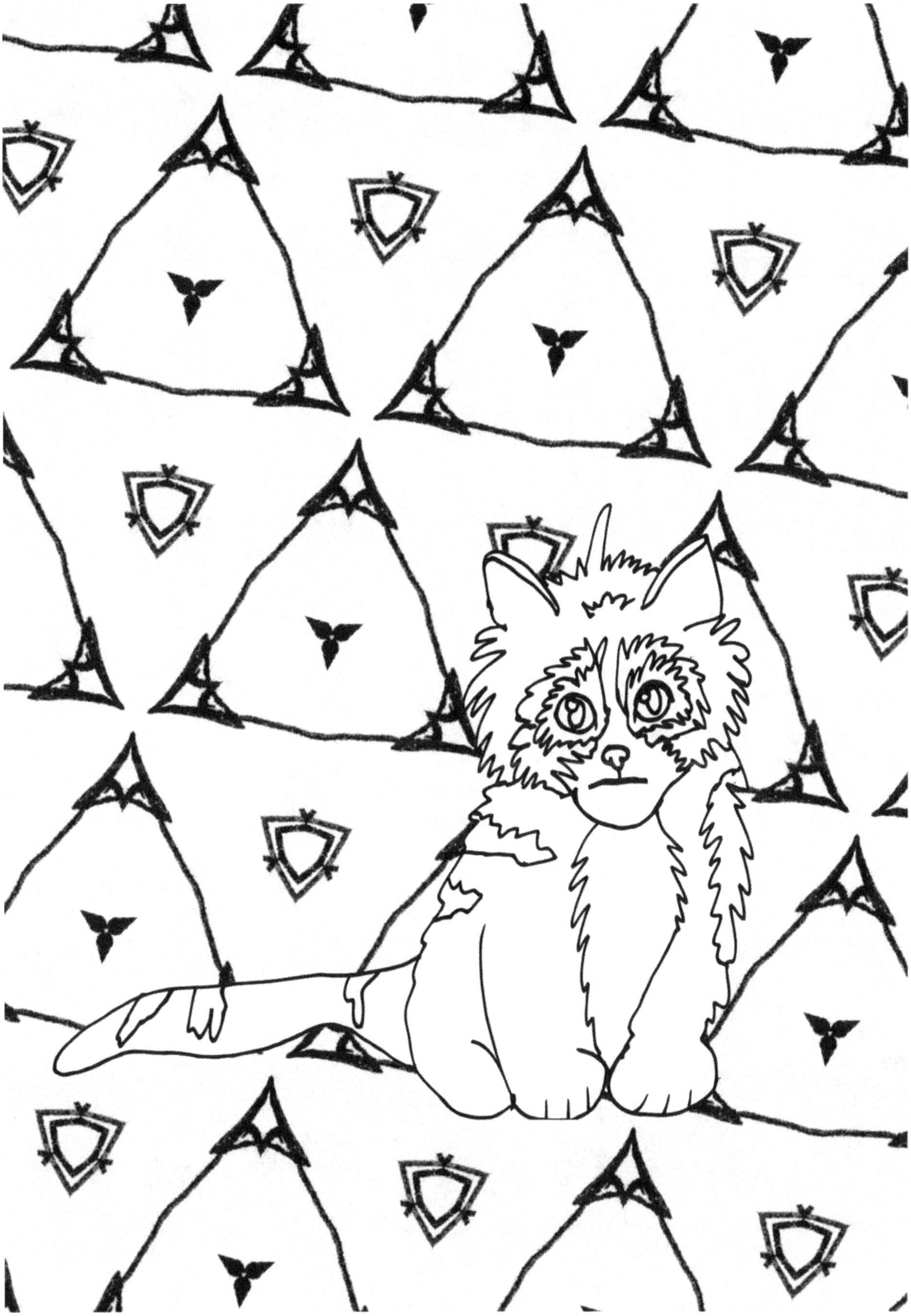

ARTIST

NAME

DATE

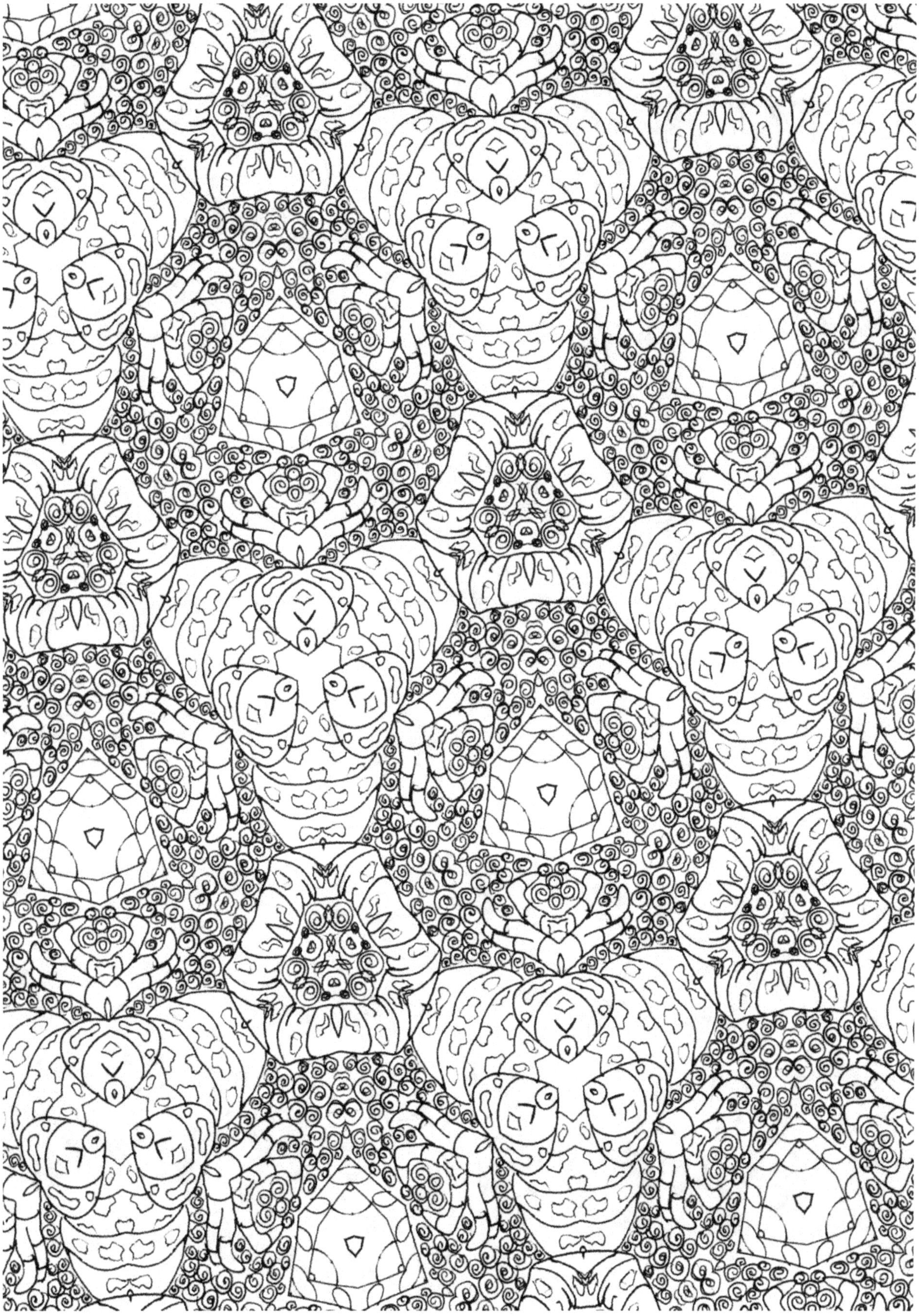

ARTIST

NAME

DATE

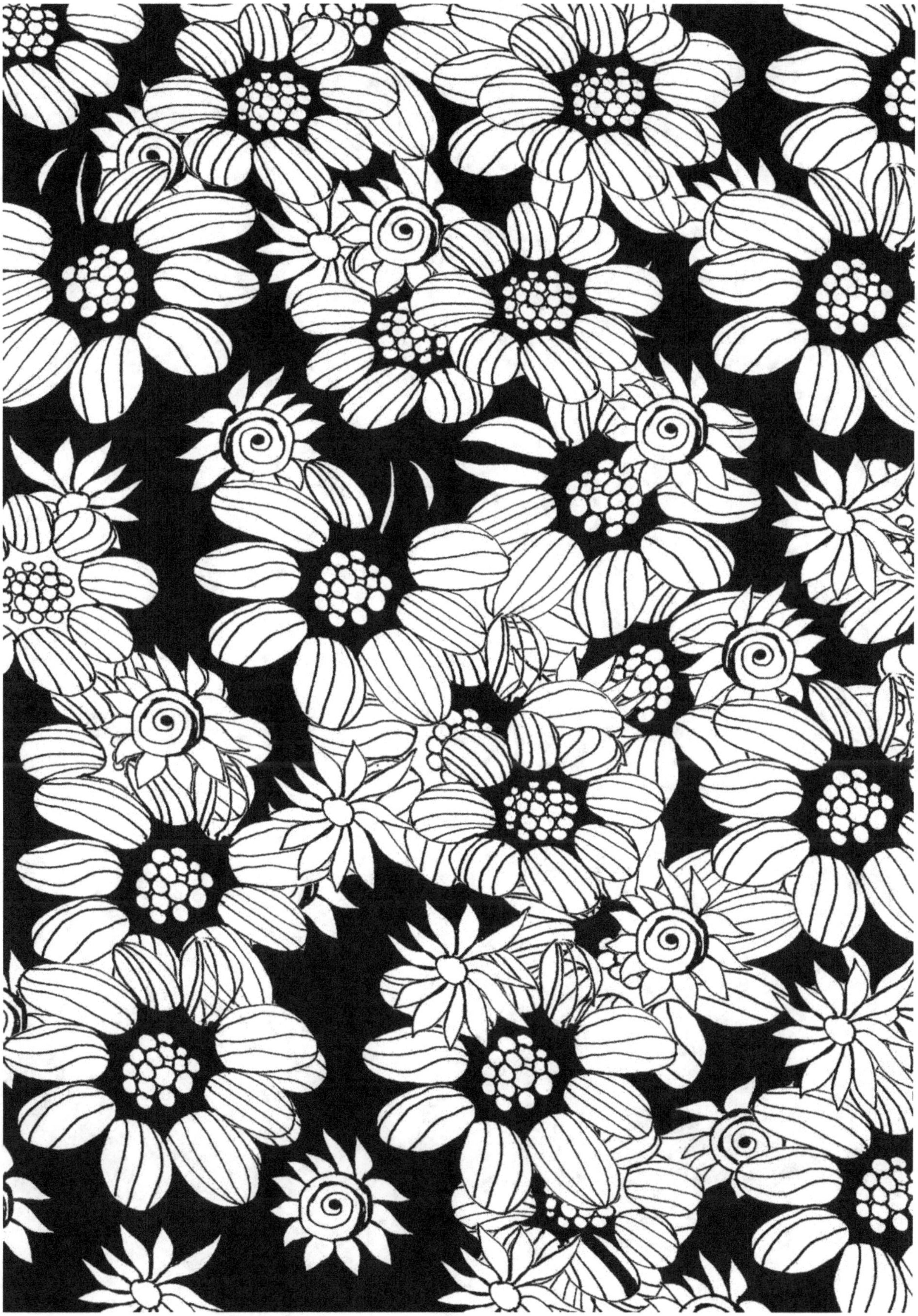

ARTIST

NAME

DATE

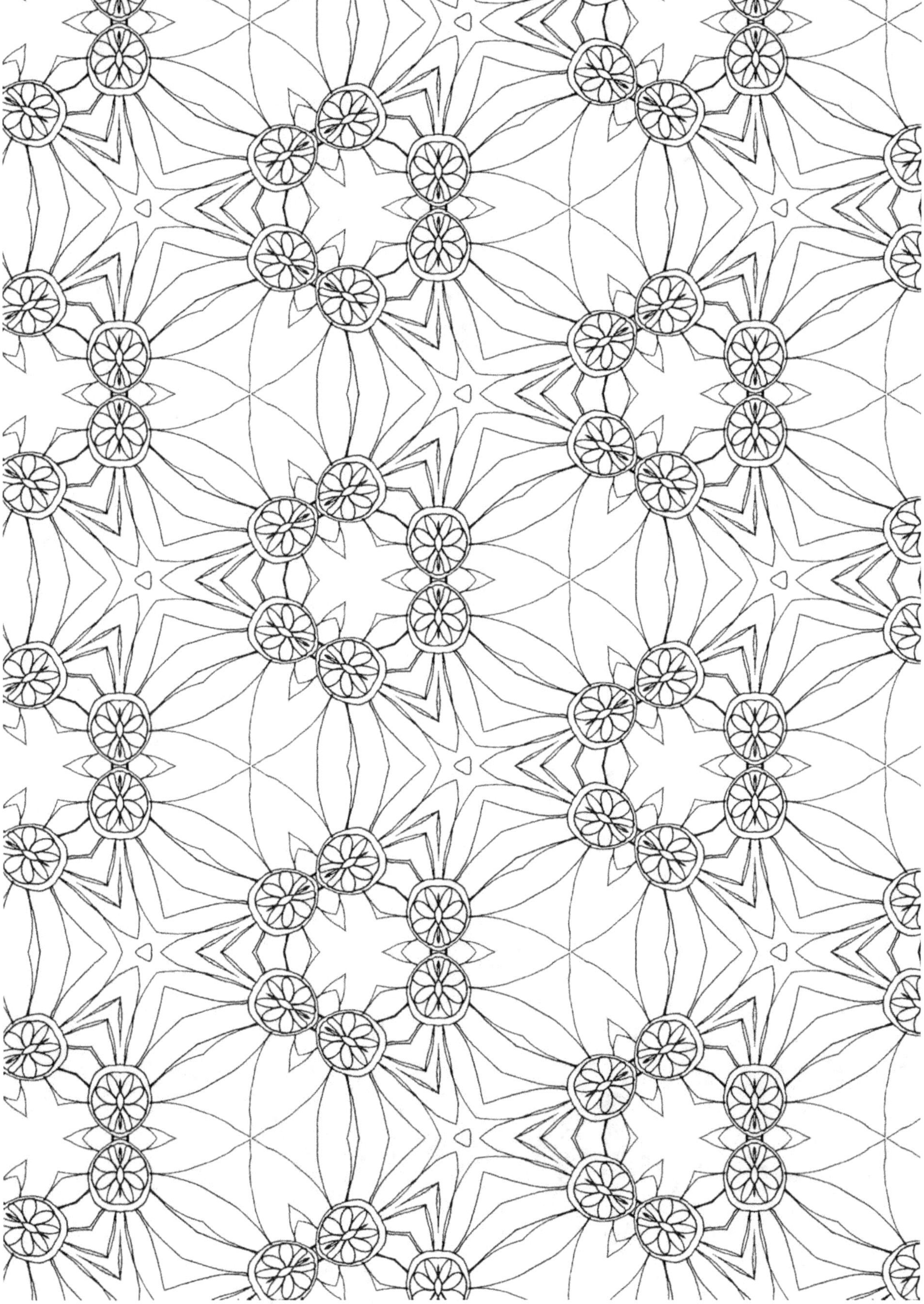

ARTIST

NAME

DATE

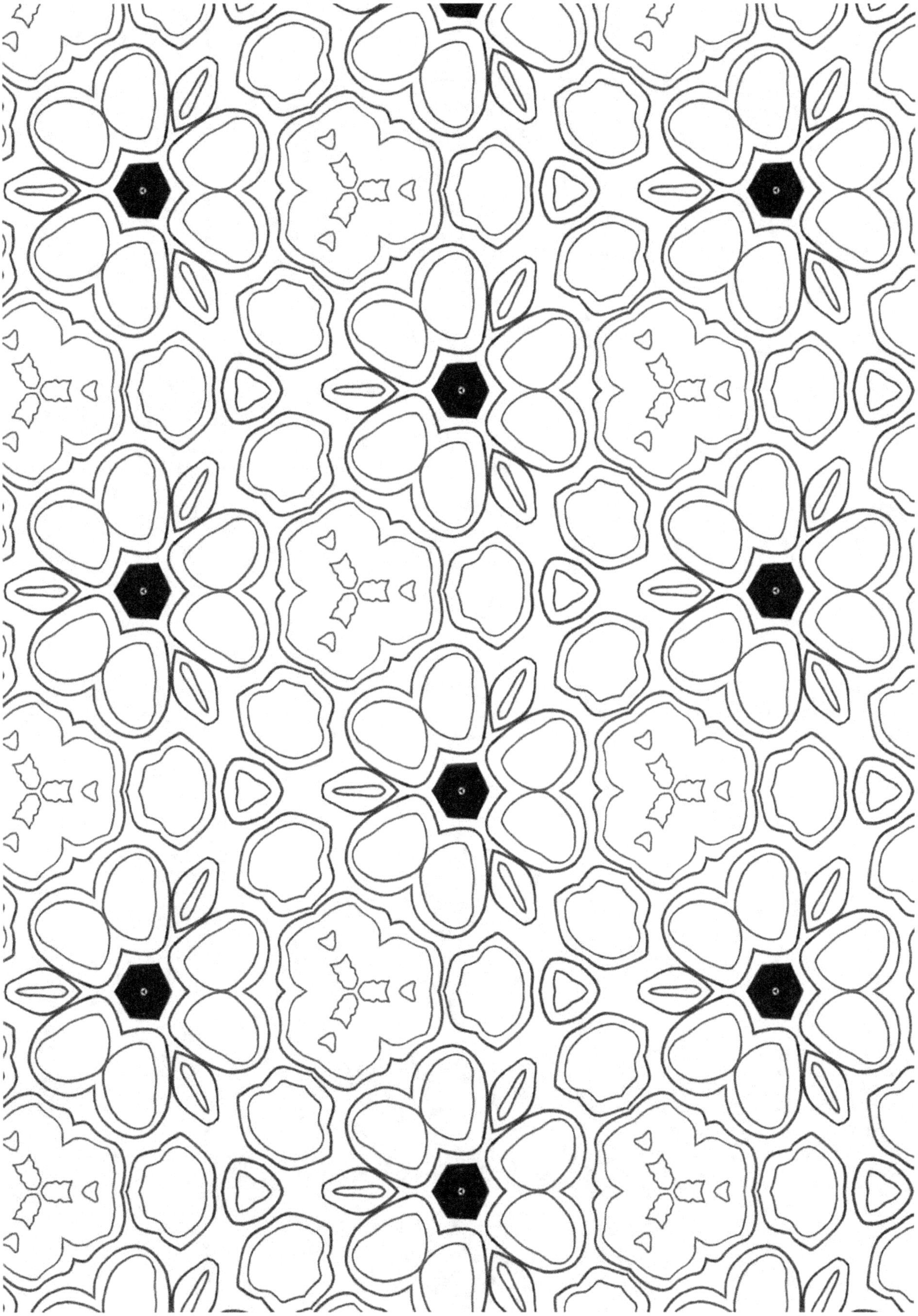

ARTIST

NAME

DATE

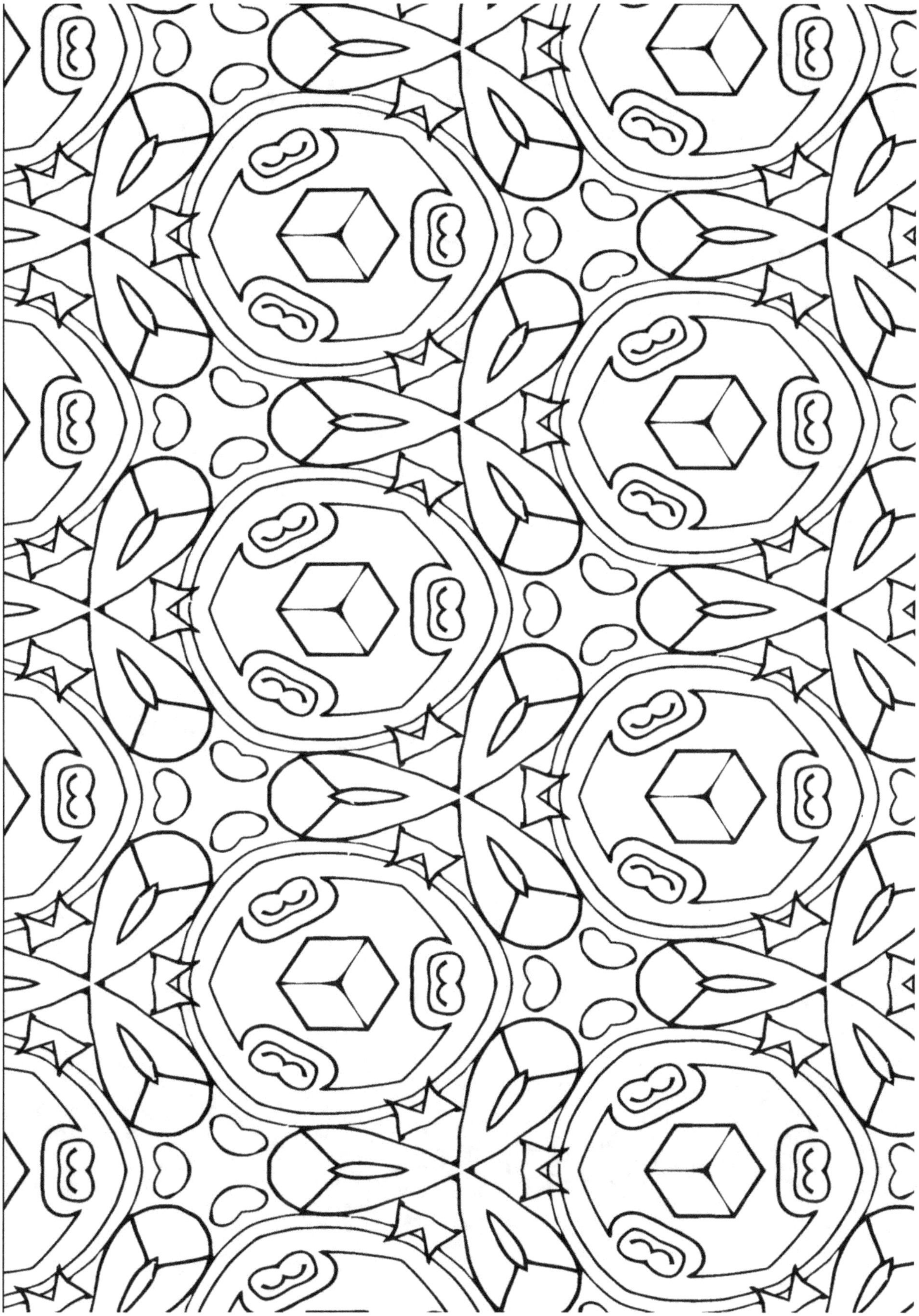

ARTIST

NAME

DATE

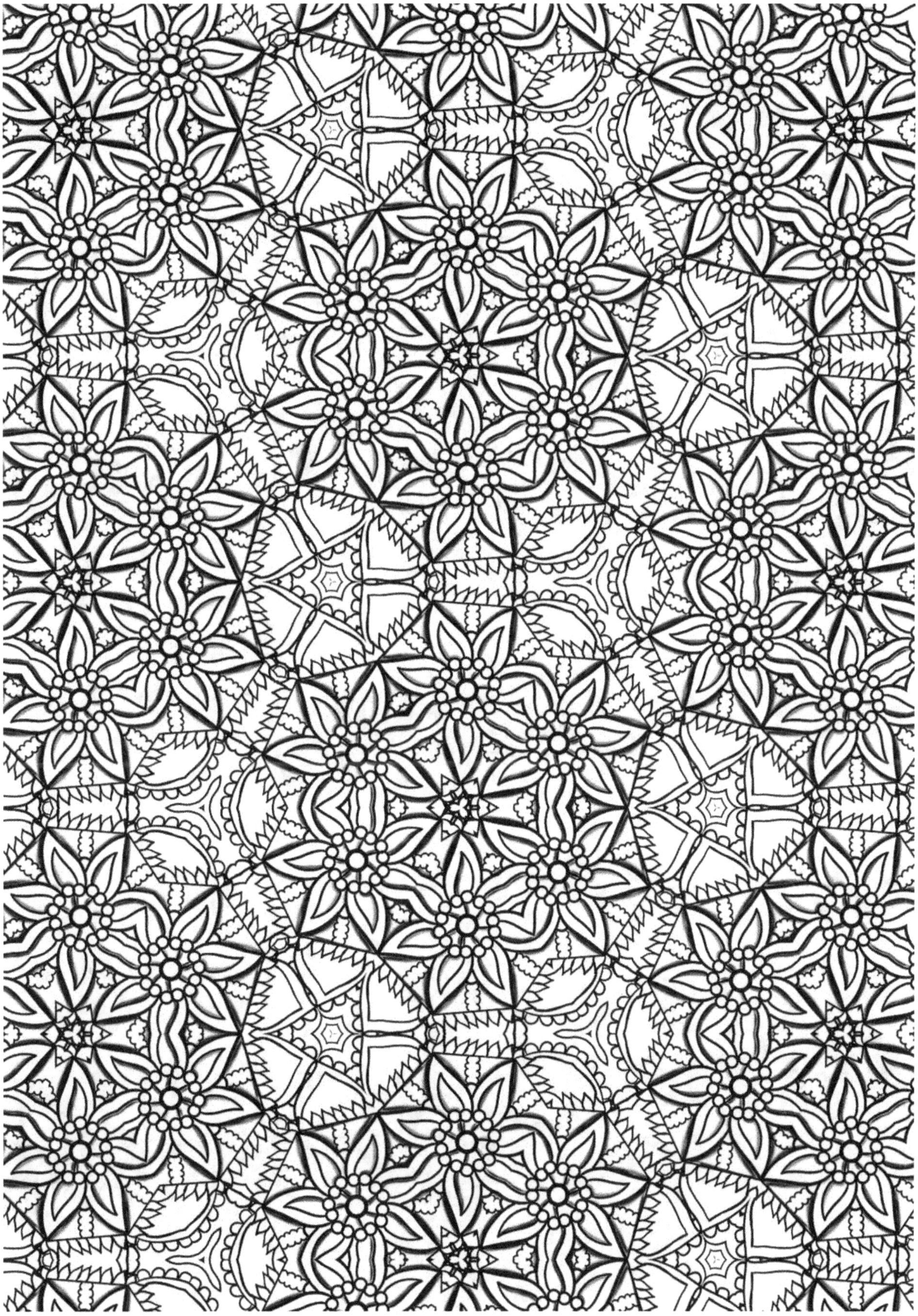

A R T I S T

NAME

DATE

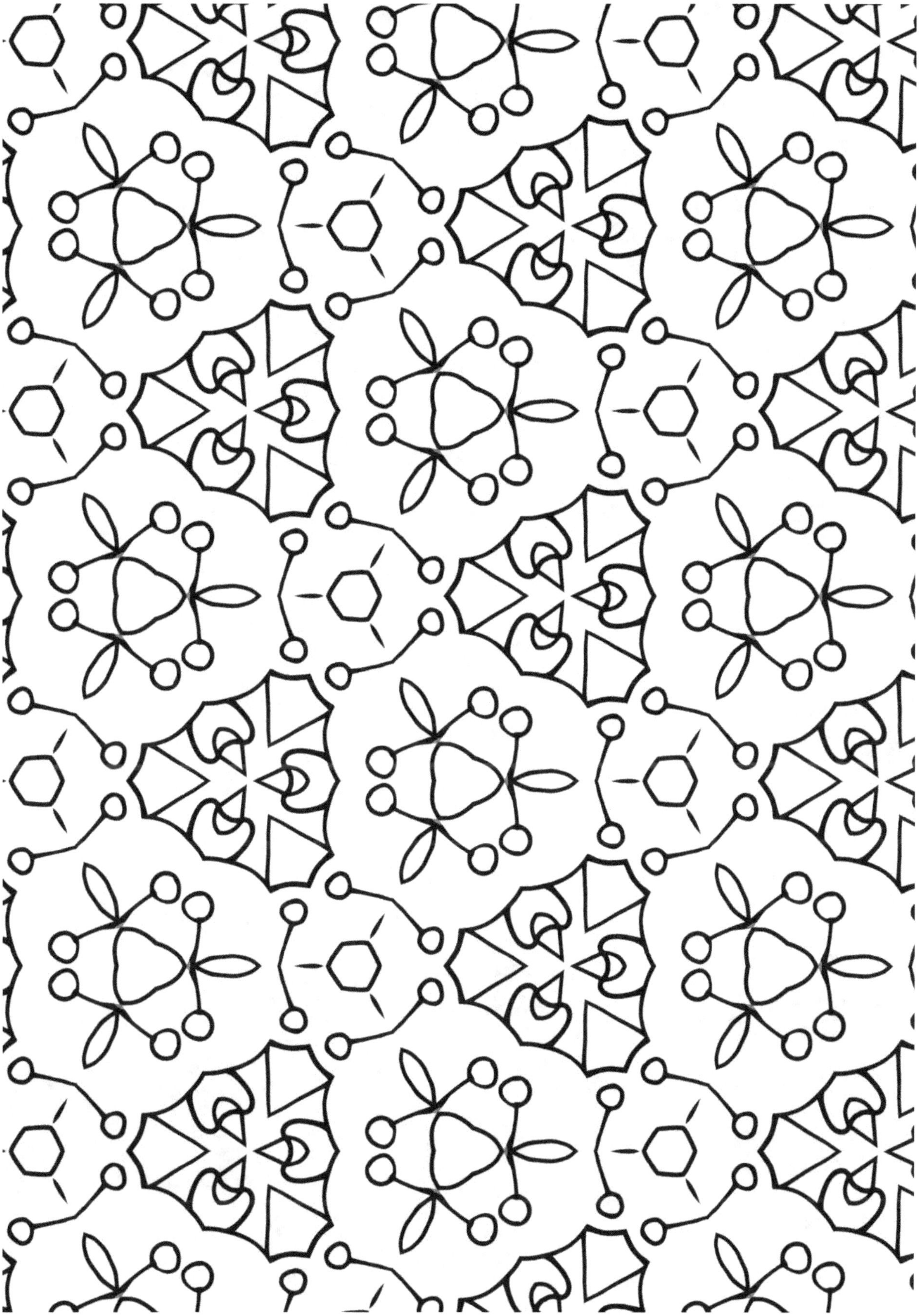

ARTIST

NAME

DATE

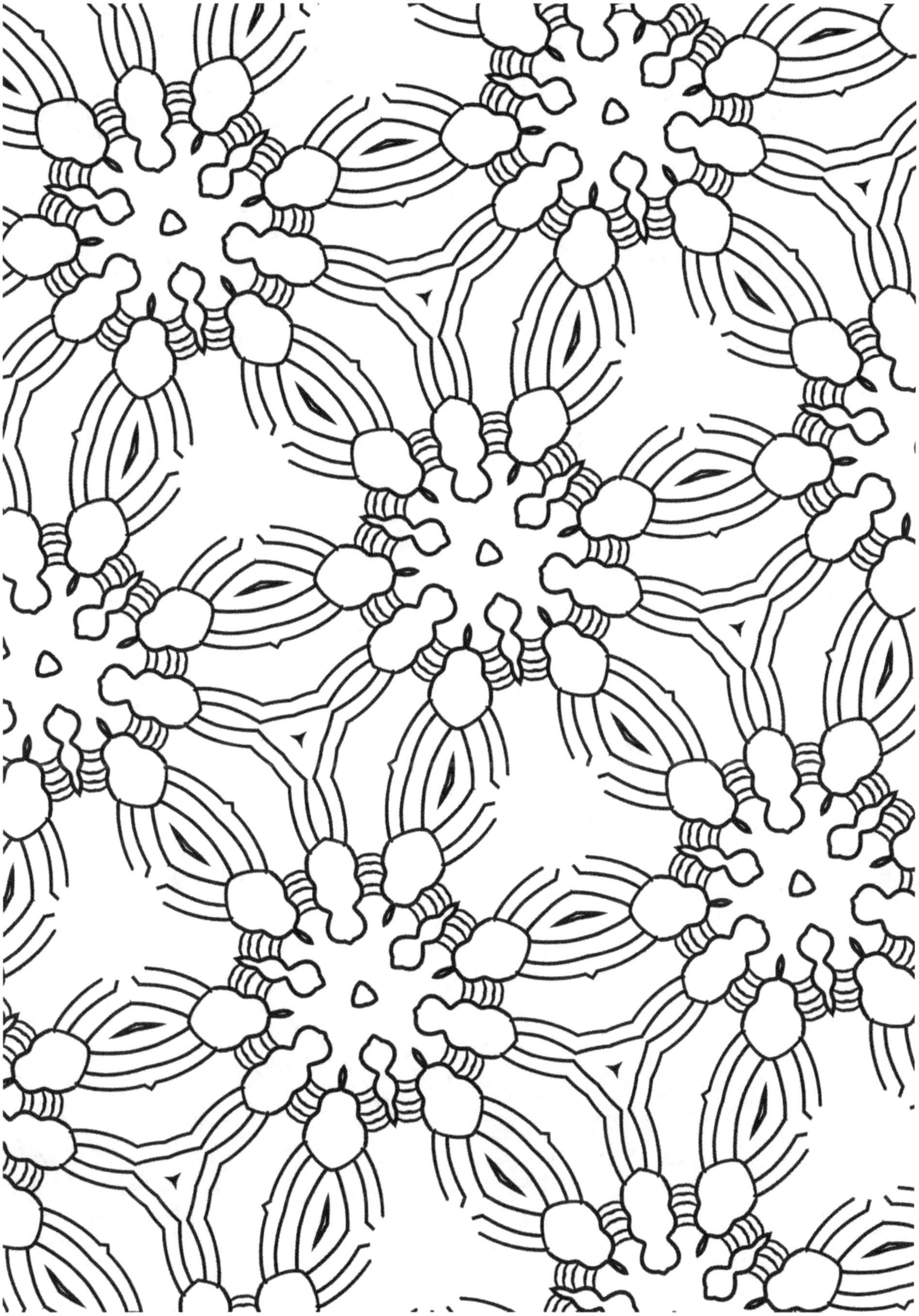

ARTIST

NAME

DATE

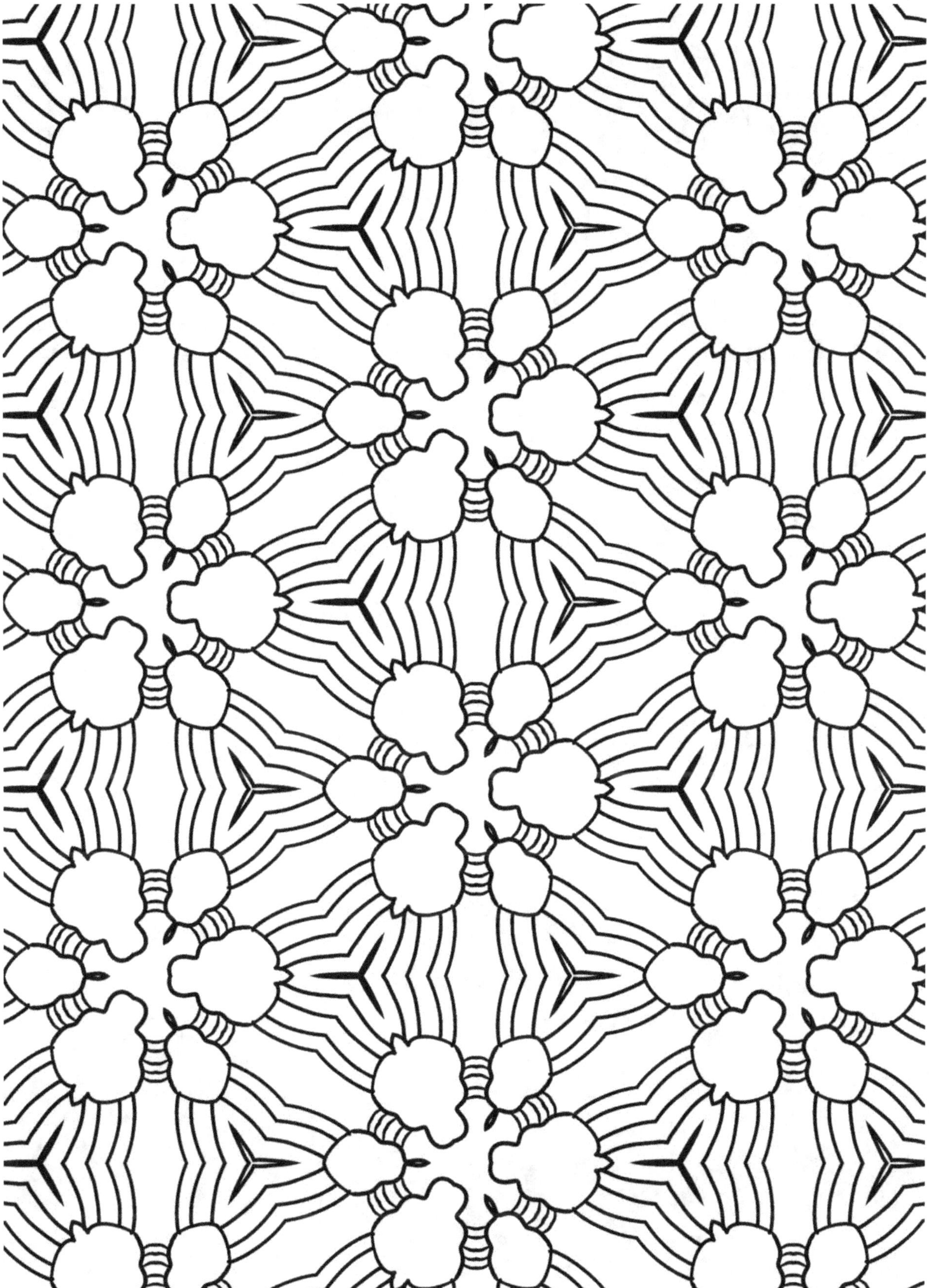

ARTIST

NAME

DATE

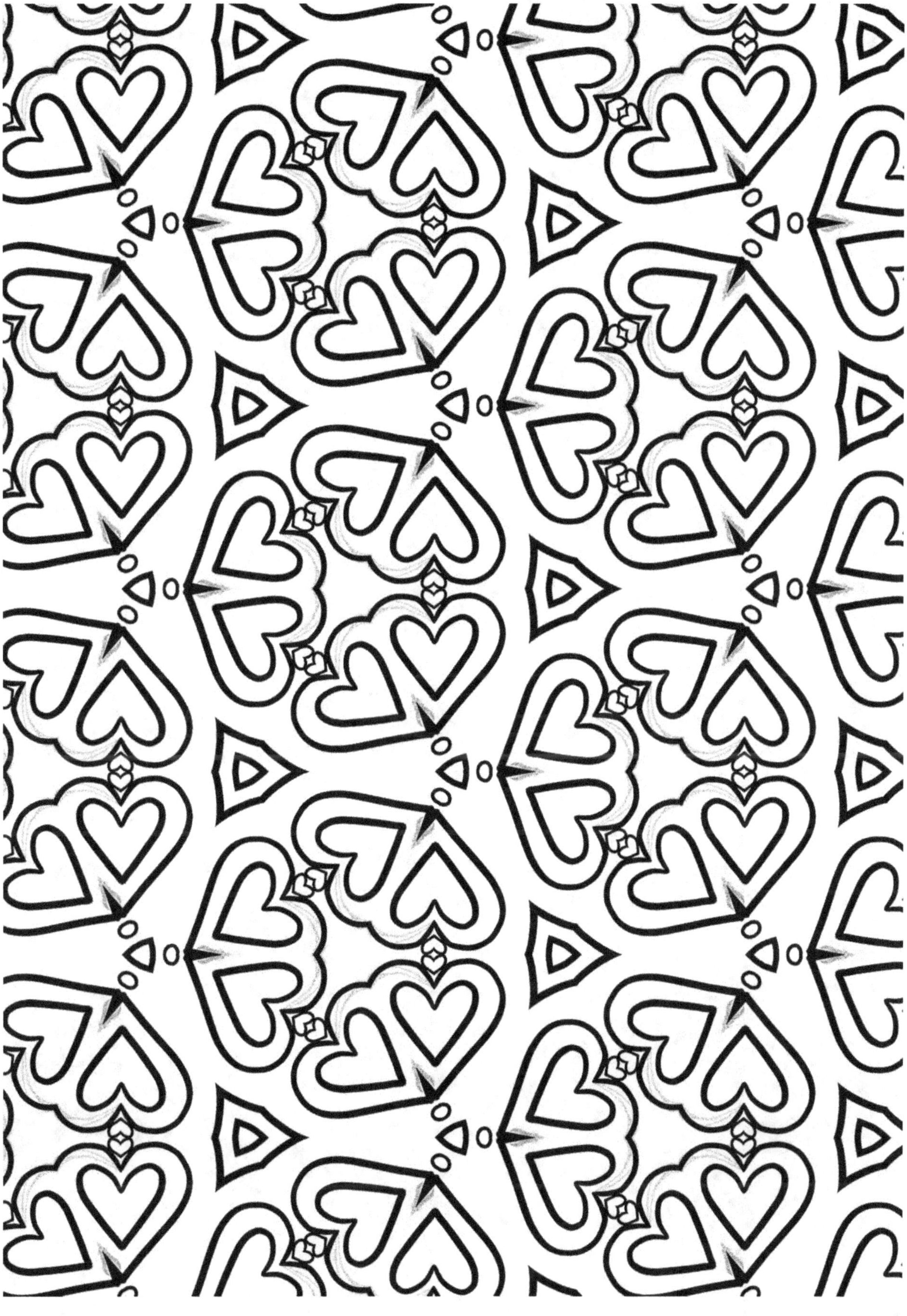

ARTIST

NAME

DATE

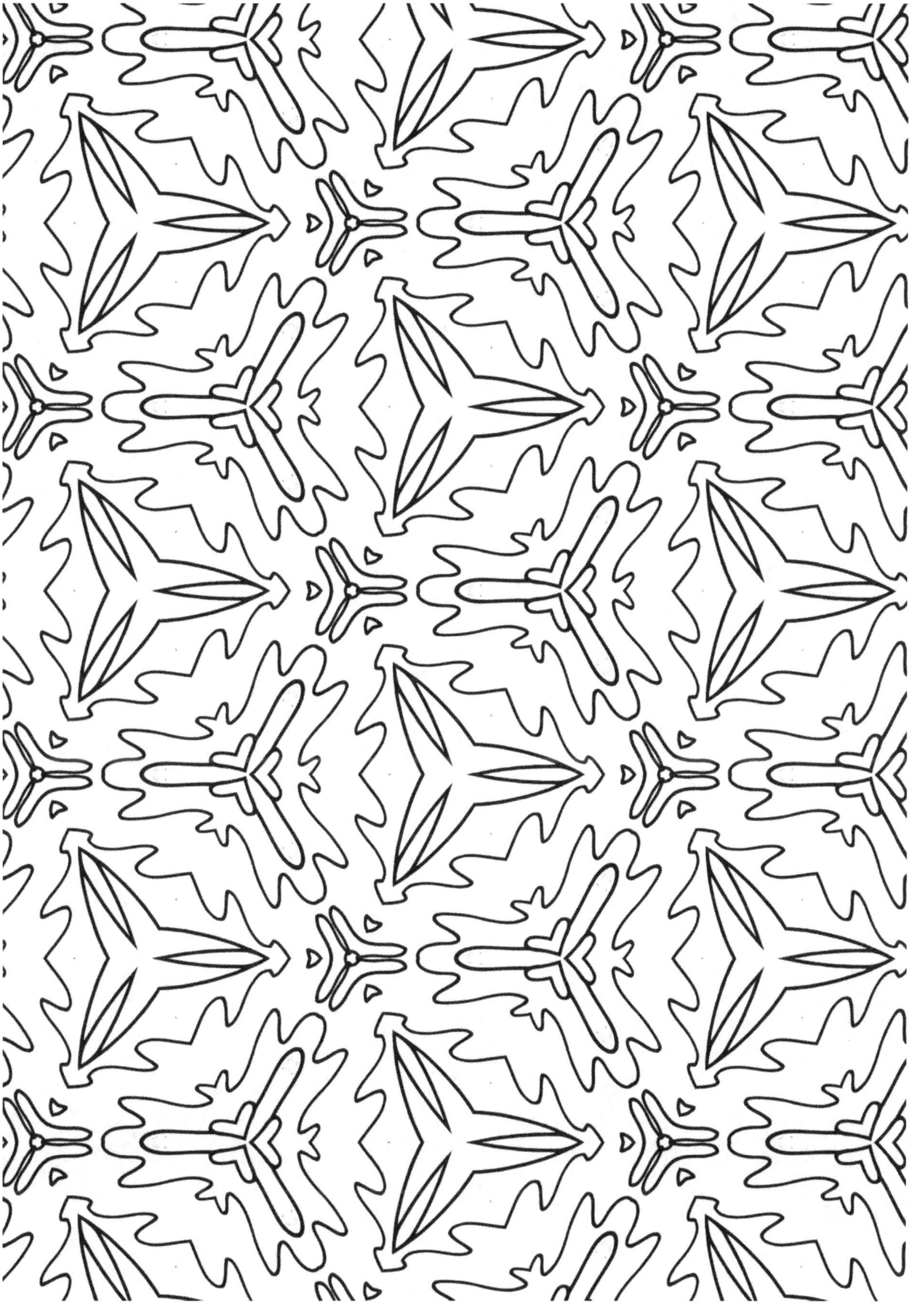

ARTIST

NAME

DATE

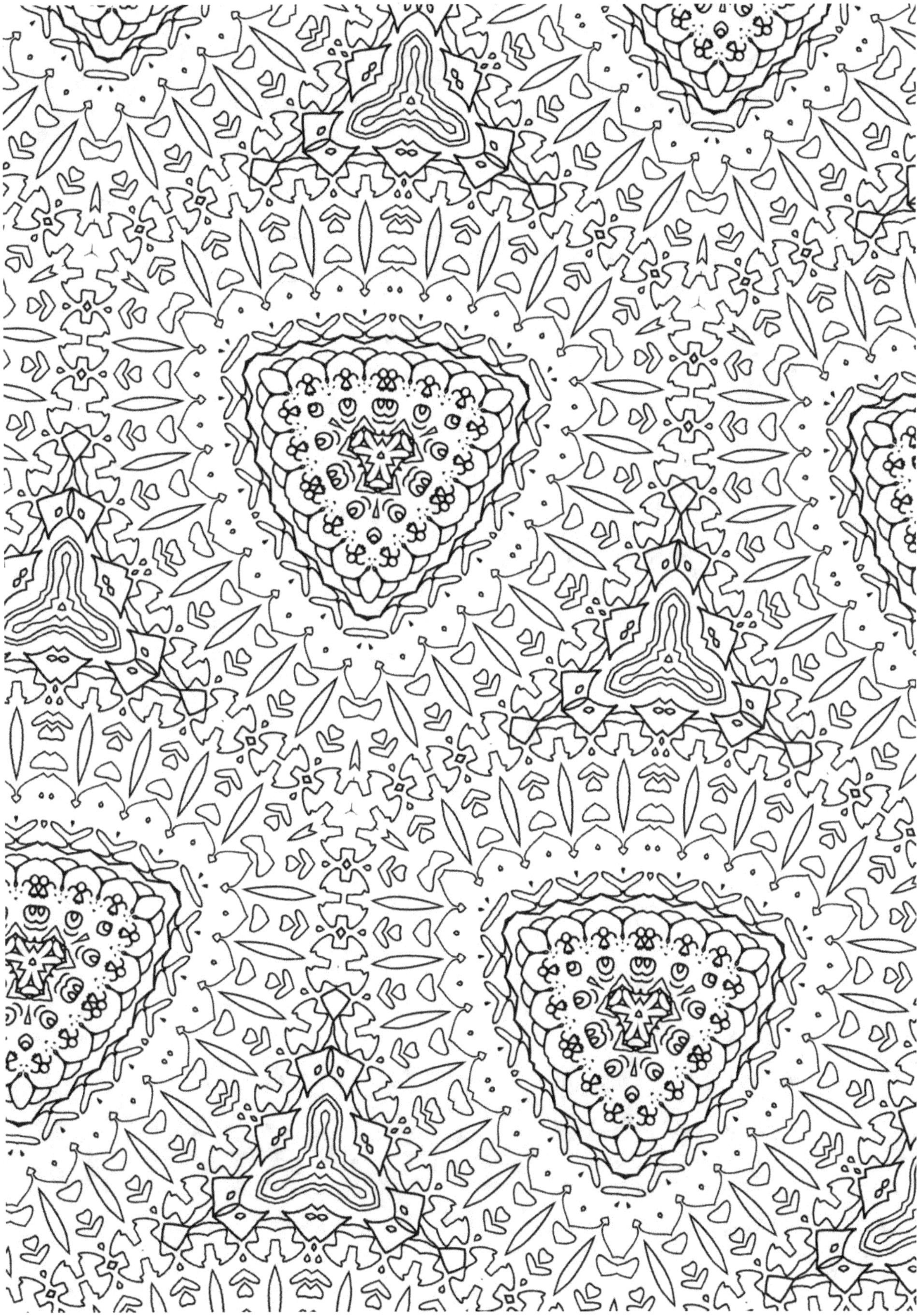

ARTIST

NAME

DATE

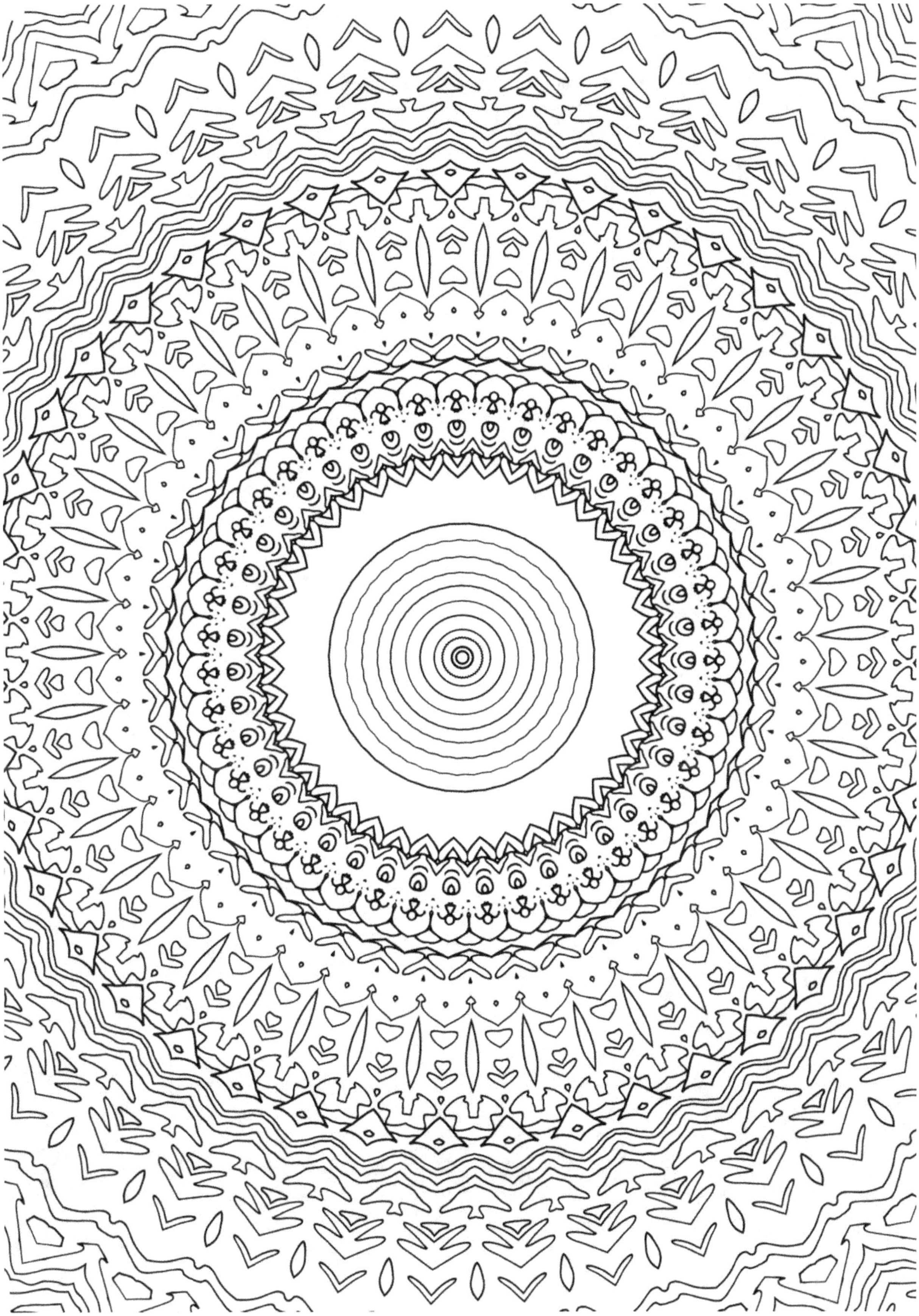

ARTIST

NAME

DATE

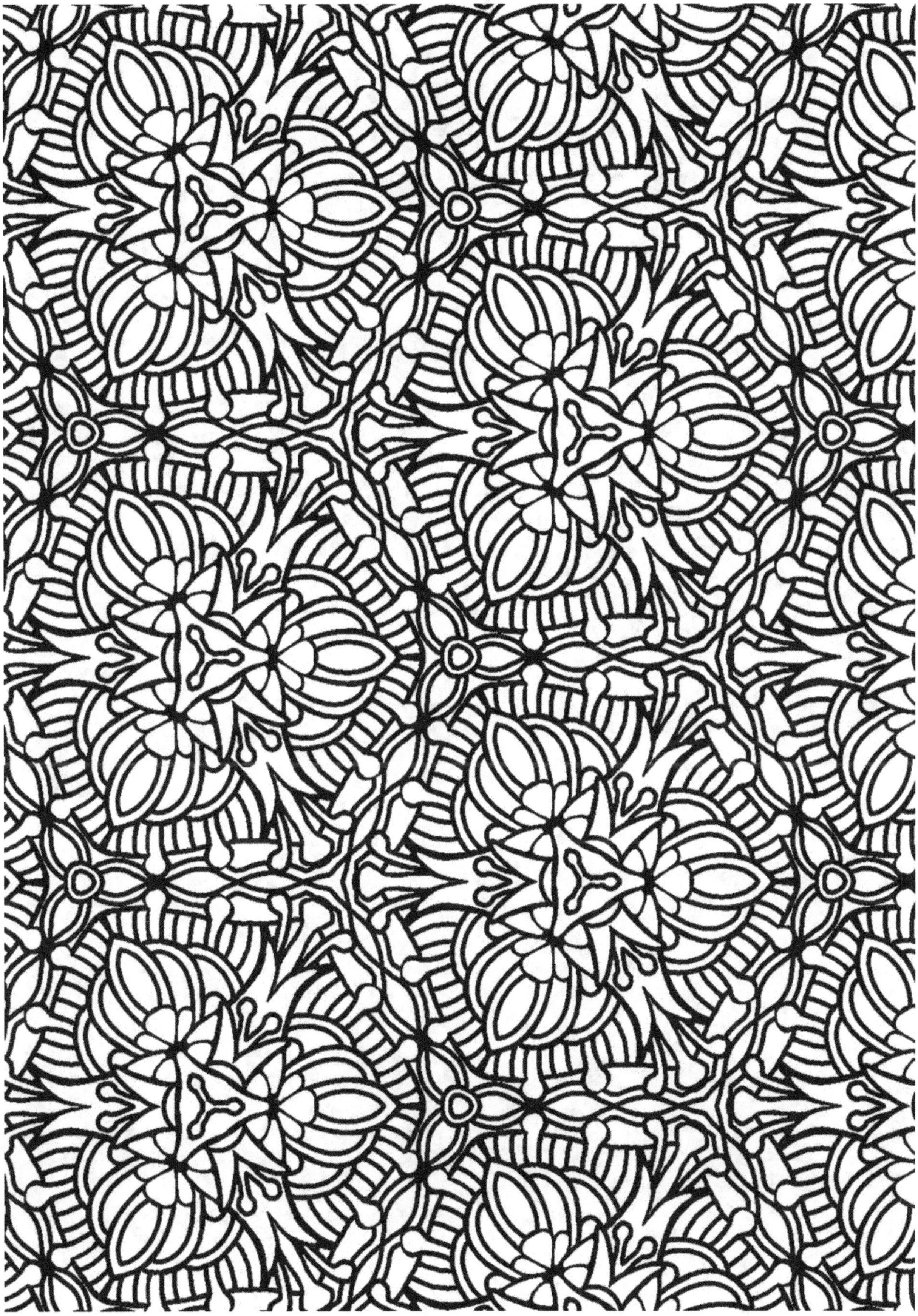

ARTIST

NAME

DATE

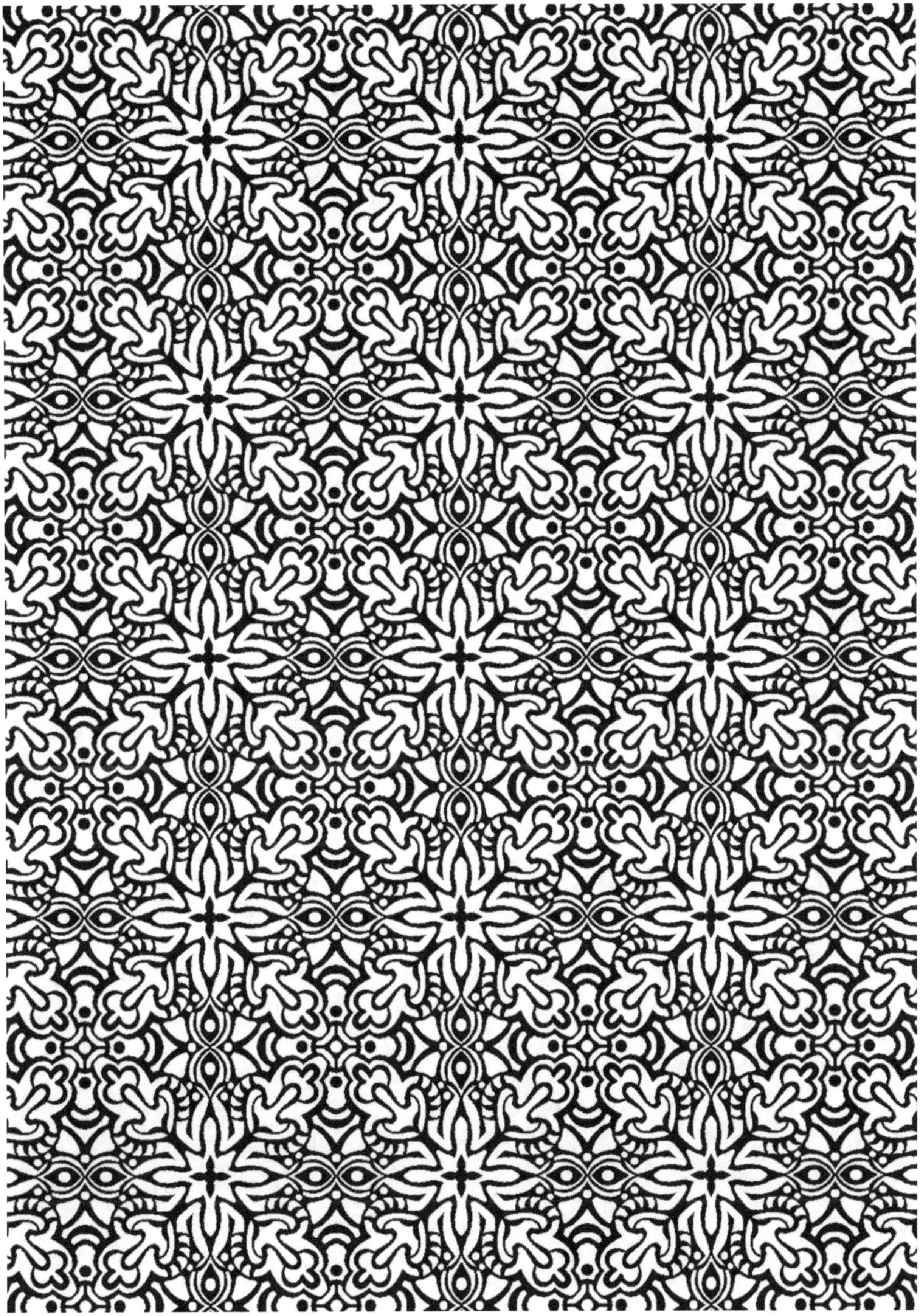

ARTIST

NAME

DATE

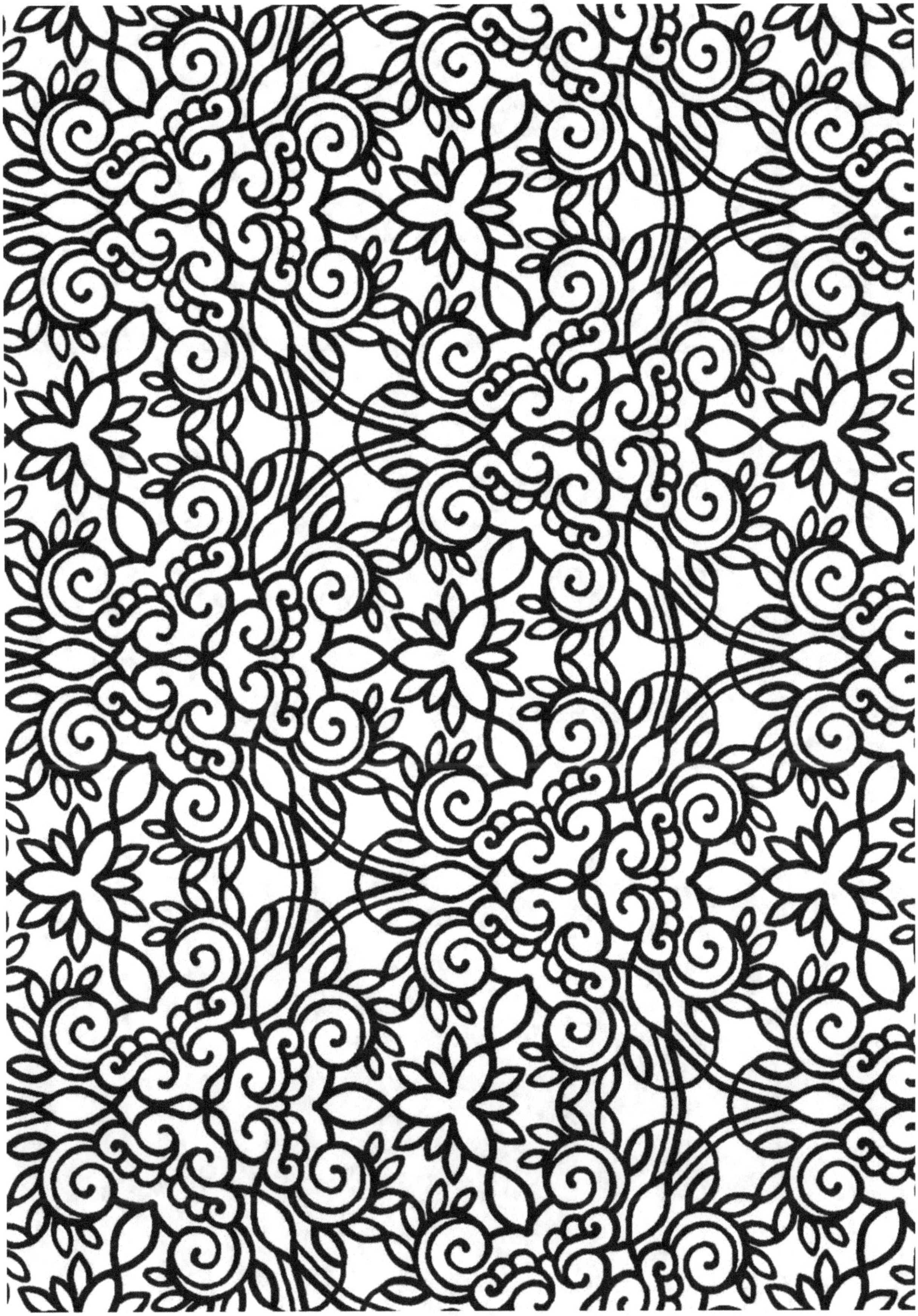

ARTIST

NAME

DATE

Artist Notes

Other Products

Please visit Jasmines author page for other coloring book titles.

www.amazon.com/author/jasminetaylor (https://goo.gl/AYQdxw)

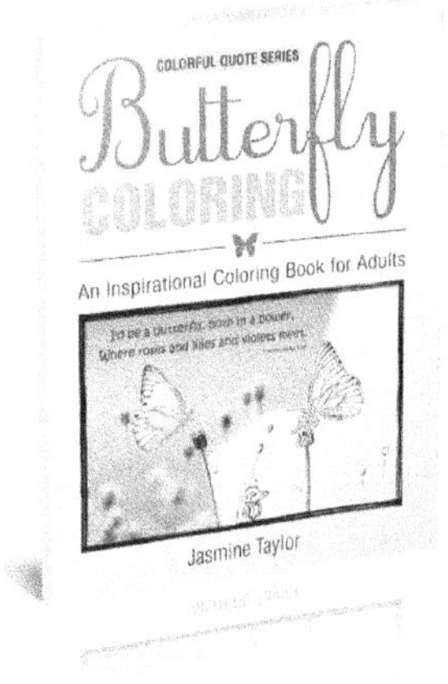

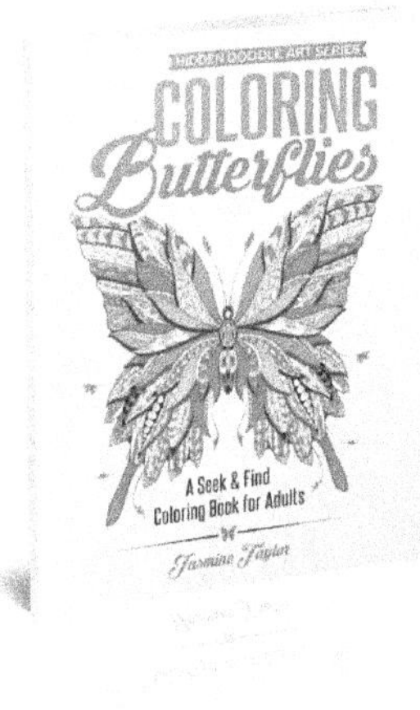

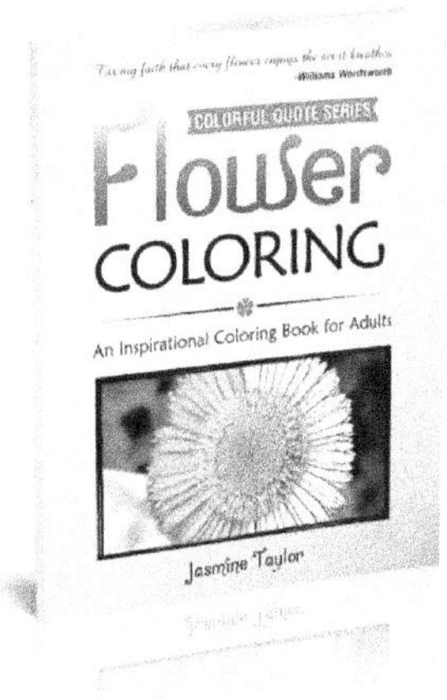

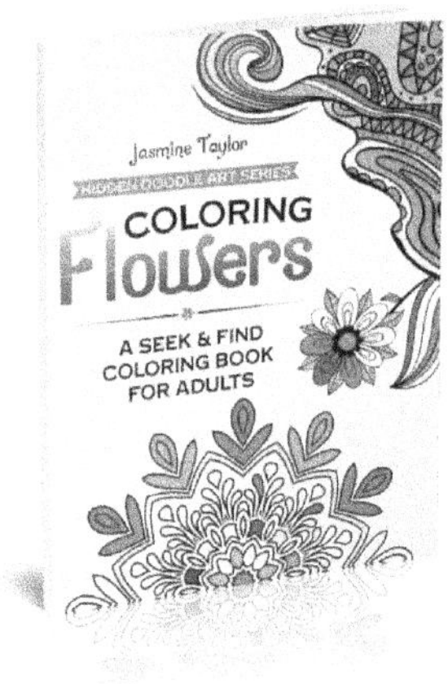

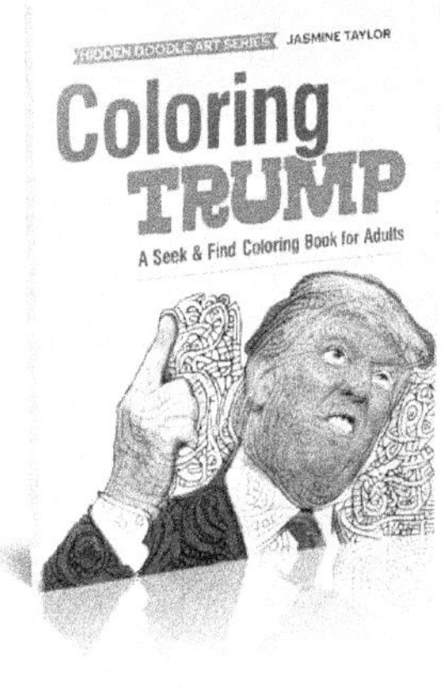

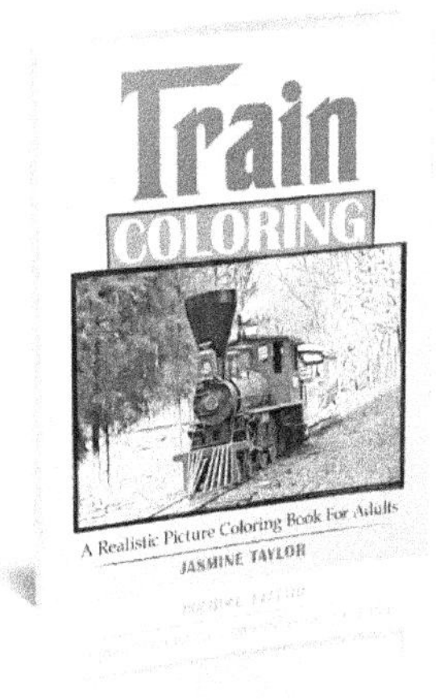

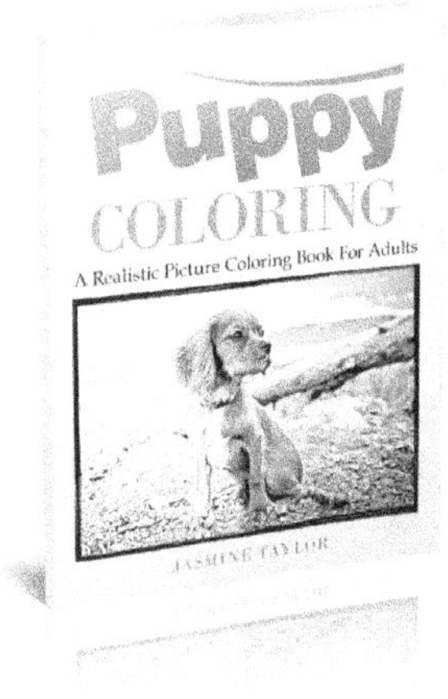

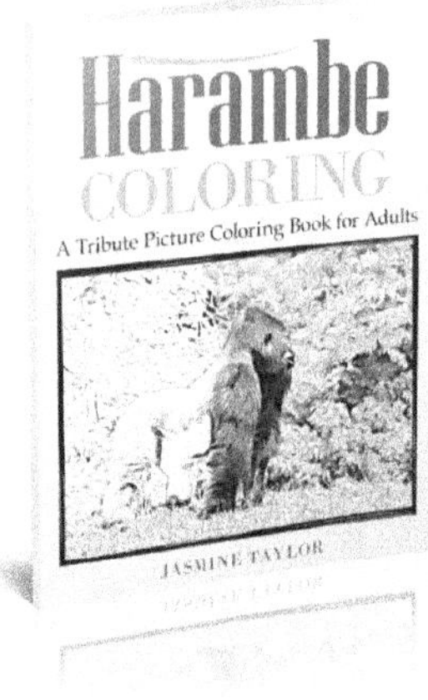

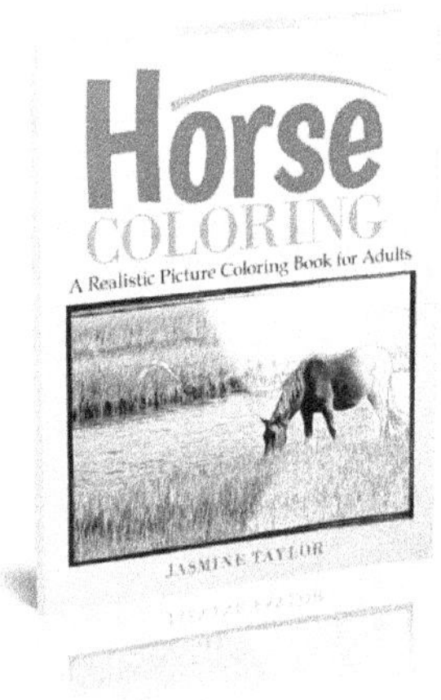

About the Author

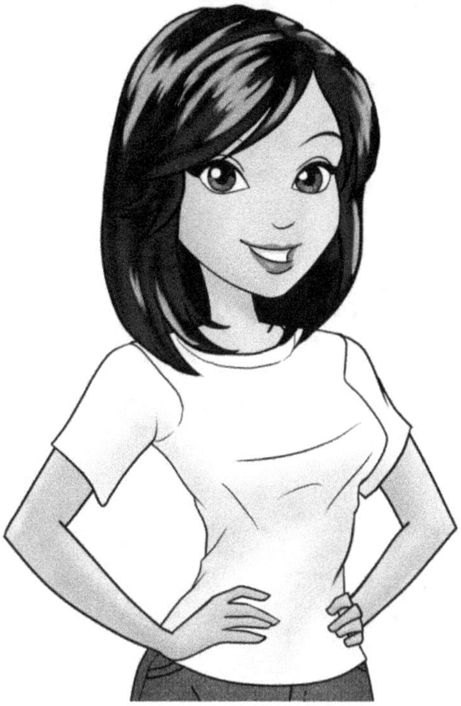

I'm passionate about art, coloring and creativity. My coloring books cover a variety of niches with varying styles and levels of difficulty from beginner to advance for all to enjoy. I'm really thrilled to offer my coloring books to you in the hope of inspiring your creative journey.

If you enjoyed this coloring book, please help others find and benefit as well by leaving a positive review on Lulu or one of its distribution partners. Thank you very much and happy coloring!

Jasmine Taylor

www.ingramcontent.com/pod-product-compliance
Lightning Source LLC
Chambersburg PA
CBHW081258180526
45170CB00007B/2473
9780359871735